Failure
to Disclose
Foreign Financial
Assets

A Tax Brief

Robert L. Sommers

SOMMERS-TAXAPEDIA.COM

ISBN-10: 0-9778616-1-9
ISBN-13: 978-0-9778616-1-3

Cover art and layout by Crawshaw Design

Sommers-Taxapedia.com

Prnted in the United States of America

About the Author

Robert L. Sommers provides sophisticated legal advice concerning complex tax, business and estate planning issues.

As an acknowledged expert in the field of tax law, Bob has written hundreds of articles, columns, and action guides and spoken at dozens of events.

Bob Sommers is The Tax Prophet. He has created and written The Tax Prophet website, a vital resource to those seeking solid U.S. tax information, issue spotting and analysis.

As a full-time practicing attorney in the heart of San Francisco's Financial District, Bob owns and operates a general tax law firm.

He focuses on U.S. and foreign individuals and small companies in the areas of

- Estate planning (wills, trusts and family-based entities)
- Foreign tax
- Business start-ups and funding
- Employee stock options
- Probate and trust administration
- Federal and California tax controversies (audits, appeals and litigation)

Certified as a Tax Specialist by the California Board of Legal Specialization of the State Bar of California (a distinction earned by less than .05% of all attorneys licensed to practice law in California,) Bob also received a postgraduate legal degree (LL.M.) in taxation from New York University School of Law in 1985, the premier graduate tax program in the U.S.

Bob has testified before the US Senate's Finance Committee regarding tax scams on the Internet. He is in demand as an expert witness in both criminal and civil cases involving Tax and Trust Law, Tax Fraud, Busted Tax Shelters, and Bogus Trust Arrangements.

The Wall Street Journal, New York Times, Forbes, CNN to Money magazine and the Best of the Web have all reviewed Bob's work and his contributions to legal education. Reviews online.

CONTENTS

Preliminary Matters

1. U.S. taxpayers[1] must report their world-wide income, credits and deductions on their U.S. tax returns (Form 1040) and, in general, are entitled to foreign tax credits for income taxed to a foreign country. If a non-resident alien, including an individual in the U.S. on an F-1 or similar visa, marries a U.S. taxpayer and they file a joint return, both must report their worldwide income and expenses. The NRA spouse is considered a U.S. resident for tax purposes, which means they need to report foreign accounts, income and gifts or inheritances (discussed below).

2. **FBARS:** Taxpayers with an ownership interest or signature authority over foreign financial accounts (bank and brokerage accounts, mutual funds, corporate, trust and other entity accounts, certain retirement plans and life insurance with a cash value) that, in the aggregate, exceed $10,000 at any time during the calendar year are required to file an annual Foreign Bank and Financial Account Report – FinCEN Form 114 (FBARS) on-line on or before June 30th of the following year. NOTE: Starting in 2017, FBARS will be due on the due date of your federal income tax return (including the extended due date, if a valid extension is filed for your income tax return). Thus, the 2016 FBAR must be filed on the due date of your 2016 federal income tax return. The maxi-

---

[1] Citizens, permanent residents (green card holders) must report their world-wide incomeregardless of where they live, others report their world-wide income if they are resident in the U.S. during the year. See Internal Revenue Code Section 7701(b) for the definition of a resident.

FAILURE TO DISCLOSE FOREIGN FINANCIAL ASSETS

mum fine for the nonwillful failure to timely file an FBAR is $10,000 and there is a six-year statute of limitations for assessment of the penalty. The penalty may be reduced or eliminated upon an affirmative showing by the taxpayer of "reasonable cause."[2]

a. The penalty for a willful failure to file an FBAR is the greater of $100,000 or 50% of the amount in the account, for each year of the violation. Since an FBAR penalty may be asserted for a maximum of six years, the penalty can be as high as $600,000 or 300% of the amount in the account, whichever is higher. Note: IRS has backed off the 300% penalty and now claims it will assess a maximum penalty of 100% on the highest open FBAR year, absent unusual circumstances meriting a higher penalty.

b. Both current and delinquent FBARs must be filed on-line: *http://bsaefiling.fincen.treas.gov/ Enroll_Individual.html.*

c. To determine the value of a foreign account, the highest value of the account during the year is multiplied by the U.S. dollar exchange rate at the end of the year, using the U.S. Treasury End-of-Year Exchange Rates. If the rate is not available, then use any recognized exchange rate service.

---

2 Circumstances that may indicate reasonable cause and good faith include an honestmisunderstanding of fact or law that is reasonable in light of all of the facts and circumstances,including the experience, knowledge, and education of the taxpayer.

FAILURE TO DISCLOSE FOREIGN FINANCIAL ASSETS

d. Strangely, IRS does not define the term "banking." In a recent unpublished decision, the Ninth Circuit Court of Appeals in U.S. v Hom, (No. 14-16214, July 26, 2016) resorted to a dictionary definition of banking and held that merely depositing funds with an on-line gambling website does not constitute banking for FBAR purposes; however, if the gambling website engages in any banking activity, such as transmitting funds to and from other banks, then the account must be reported on an FBAR.

3. **Willfulness:** Willfulness is the central concept in the foreign income and reporting arena. The term "willfulness" is defined as the voluntary, intentional violation of a known legal duty. United States v. Pomponio, 429 U.S. 10, and the burden of proof is on the government. Conversely, non-willful conduct is conduct that is due to negligence, inadvertence, or mistake or conduct that is the result of a good faith misunderstanding of the requirements of the law.

a. Usually, for willfulness to occur there needs to be an overt act of evading taxes, such as using tax haven companies or secret bank accounts, sending false or misleading documents to a foreign bank or to a tax preparer, using the funds on a regular basis, including on trips abroad, using an ATM to withdraw funds or a debit card to access the account, or diverting taxable income from the U.S. system.

FAILURE TO DISCLOSE FOREIGN FINANCIAL ASSETS

b. In this regard, taxpayers need to review every transaction involving their foreign accounts, such as deposits, withdrawals, transfers between accounts, opening and closing of accounts and transfers of funds to the U.S. or outside the country where the account is located, and whether any funds were held in trusts or entities or by other family members to hide the true source of the funds.

c. The problem with a self-diagnosing willfulness is that, invariably, a taxpayer will decide that he/she was not willful in their mind ("Gee, I didn't mean to exclude the income or account..."). Unfortunately, willfulness can be established by both direct and circumstantial evidence, so taxpayers should seek out the guidance of an experience tax professional willing to ask probing questions to determine whether willfulness exists in their situation.

4. **Form 8938:** In addition to the FBAR requirement, starting in 2011 taxpayers with foreign financial account and certain other financial assets, generally, bank and brokerage accounts, individually held stock, securities or interests in foreign entities (including family owned entities), and certain employee stock benefit plans, must report those assets on Form 8938, which is filed with the Form 1040. Accounts listed on FBARS are also included on this Form (except accounts where the individual only has signature authority).

FAILURE TO DISCLOSE FOREIGN FINANCIAL ASSETS

There are minimum thresholds that apply, depending on whether taxpayers are single or joint filers and whether they live in the U.S.. The penalty for failure to file Form 8938 is $10,000 per delinquent filing and the assessment period is generally three years. The penalty may be eliminated upon an affirmative showing of reasonable cause.

5. **Foreign Corporate Ownership:** Taxpayers with a 10% or greater interest in a foreign corporation who have engaged in certain transactions with the corporation during the year must file Form 5471 with Form 1040. This form contains substantial detail about the foreign corporation. The penalty for failure to file Form 5471 is $10,000 per filing failure and the assessment period does not expire. The penalty may be eliminated upon an affirmative showing of reasonable cause.

6. **Foreign Partnership or LLC Ownership:** Taxpayers with a 10% or greater ownership in a foreign partnership of LLC are obligated to file Form 8865 when they engage in transfers to the partnership, acquire ownership that triggers the 10% threshold and in other situations involving changes in ownership and dispositions of partnership interests or assets. The penalty for failure to file Form 8865 is $10,000 per filing failure and the assessment period does not expire. The penalty may be eliminated upon an affirmative showing of reasonable cause.

FAILURE TO DISCLOSE FOREIGN FINANCIAL ASSETS

7. Gifts or Inheritances: Taxpayers who receive a gift or inheritance from a foreign individual[3] of $100,000 or more during the calendar year must file Form 3520. The due date is the same as the Form 1040, and is extended if a valid extension is filed for the Form 1040. The threshold reporting requirement for a gift or inheritance from an entity or trust is much lower.[4] The penalty for failing to file Form 3520 is 5% for each month that the failure occurs, to a maximum of 25%. The penalty may be eliminated upon an affirmative showing of reasonable cause.

---

3 Receiving a foreign gift or inheritance from the U.S. individual or entity is not subject to Form 3520 reporting.

4 The reporting requirement threshold for a gift or inheritance from a non-individual is $15,601 in 2015 and is adjusted annually for inflation.

Choices Available for Failing to Timely Report Foreign Income or Filing Information Forms

There are several alternatives available for taxpayers who have unreported income or have not filed one or more of the foreign information forms – FBARS, Form 8938, Form 5471 or 8865 and Form 3520 (collectively "Information Forms").

1. **Do Nothing:** Taxpayers can ignore their past transgressions and hope IRS never finds out about the failure(s). With the new information reporting regimes implemented by IRS involving foreign banks, known ad FATCA (Foreign Account Tax Compliance Act), U.S. taxpayer information may be furnished by the foreign banks to IRS, so this option is not feasible as a practical matter.

2. **File the Delinquent Forms:** File the delinquent forms and amended tax returns to report omitted foreign income, and attach reasonable cause explanations to the delinquent Information Forms. Under this option, the taxpayer comes clean, voluntarily discloses his/her foreign assets and pays taxes on foreign income. Although there is no legal protection for penalties and potential criminal prosecution, as a practical matter, IRS seldom asserts significant penalties, especially when the actions were not willful. This might be the only alternative when a taxpayer does not qualify for one of the IRS disclosure programs.

3. **Special Exception for Filing Delinquent Information Forms:** If taxpayers have fully disclosed their foreign

FAILURE TO DISCLOSE FOREIGN FINANCIAL ASSETS

income on their U.S. tax return, but failed to file one or more Information Forms, IRS has a special exception that allows the delinquent forms to be filed with a reasonable cause explanation attached. If this occurs, IRS will not penalize the delinquent filing. In a recent update, IRS states that the forms can be filed even if there are unpaid taxes, but it reserves the right to reject the reasonable cause explanation.

4. **Enter into the IRS's Offshore Voluntary Disclosure Program (OVDP):** This program is intended for those who willfully failed to file Information Forms or report their foreign income, amounting to potential criminal tax fraud or evasion violations. Under OVDP, taxpayers must file eight (8) years of FBARS, amend their returns for eight (8) years, paying all the taxes and interest owing, plus a 20% negligence penalty and supply IRS with foreign account information. In addition, tax-payers must pay a fine equal to 27.5% of the highest value in their unreported foreign accounts over the past eight years.[5] In reality, because of the fluctuations in asset values, the fine might be closer to 40-50% of current assets. In return, there would be no penalties for Information Forms and no criminal prosecution. This harsh penalty renders OVDP financially impractical, except when there are criminal tax fraud or eva-

---

[5] The penalty climbs to 50% if a taxpayer used bank or financial institution considered by IRS to be criminal; even if just a small portion of the overseas funds were held in such a bank the 50% penalty rate applies to all foreign accounts.

FAILURE TO DISCLOSE FOREIGN FINANCIAL ASSETS

sion involved, or the amounts in the foreign accounts are relatively modest compared to the potential penalties.

5. OVDP is recommended when a taxpayer has affirmatively misled a bank or financial institution regarding his/her U.S. residency, has made systematic withdrawals from the account or has misled the government or a tax preparer regarding income from, or the existence of, foreign accounts. Also, OVDP is appropriate when there is unreported income from purchases or sales of foreign real estate, the operation of a business or other large payments (such as exercise of stock options or bonuses).

6. **Streamlined Disclosure Procedures:** In June, 2014 IRS announced a new program for taxpayers willing to certify under federal laws of perjury, that they were not willful in their violations of the Information Return filing requirements.

   a. DOMESTIC STREAMLINED: Instead of a 27.5% penalty, taxpayer pay a fine of 5% of the highest amount reported on: (i) six (6) years of FBARS or (ii) the latest three (3) years on Form 8938, Thus, one compares the FBAR amount for each tax year for six years, with the Form 8938 amounts for the latest three (3) years and uses the higher of the two to calculate the 5% penalty. In addition, taxpayers file three (3) years of amended returns, attaching delinquent Information

FAILURE TO DISCLOSE FOREIGN FINANCIAL ASSETS

Forms, file 6 years of FBARS on line and file Form 3520 (if there was an unreported foreign gift or inheritance) as well.

b. FOREIGN STREAMLINED: For taxpayers with a permanent abode (principal residence, whether owned or rented) outside the U.S. and in at one or more of the most recent three years for which the U.S. tax return due date (or properly applied for extended due date) has passed have not been physically present in the U.S. for more than 35 days, the 5% penalty is eliminated under the foreign streamlined program. Note: If a joint return was filed, then both spouses must meet the 35-day test in the same calendar year.

c. With respect to both the domestic and foreign streamlined programs, there is a potentially huge pitfall: taxpayers must sign a certification, under federal laws of perjury, that they were not willful and if IRS concludes otherwise, the streamlined procedures are voided and taxpayers could face criminal prosecution, with the certification used as evidence against them or as an additional criminal charge of perjury – so the stakes are incredibly high, especially when a taxpayer indicated on his/her tax return that there were no foreign accounts and if there is

FAILURE TO DISCLOSE FOREIGN FINANCIAL ASSETS

significant unreported foreign income.

i. The certification of non-willfulness must set forth detailed facts stating that failure to file tax returns, report all income, pay all tax, and submit all required information returns, including FBARs, resulted from non-willful conduct and giving the specific reasons why their conduct should be considered non-willful.

ii. For example, taxpayers who have misled their foreign banks regarding their U.S. taxpayer status, misled their tax preparers regarding foreign income or assets, used an ATM to withdraw funds from the foreign account, received cash payments overseas and deposited the funds in a foreign or U.S. bank account without reporting the income, should think long and hard about whether signing a certification under penalties of perjury that they were non-willful. A detailed outline of factors to consider and reasons why a taxpayer might be non-willful is attached as Appendix "A" and sample explanations are attached as Appendix "B."

7. **Transitional Relief:** Taxpayers who entered into OVDP before June, 2014 and believe they meet the new non-willfulness standards, may request transitional relief. If

FAILURE TO DISCLOSE FOREIGN FINANCIAL ASSETS

IRS grants the request, the fine drops to 5%, if the request is denied, the taxpayer remains in the OVDP program, but retains the right to opt-out and take their chances in a full IRS audit.

Examples of the Decision Points:

Assume a taxpayer, Vinny, a permanent resident (green card holder) living in the U.S. has $1.5 million in a foreign bank account, earns $30,000 a year in foreign interest and has filed his Form 1040 income tax return, but has not included Form 8938 or his foreign income. In addition, Vinny has not filed FBARS. His foreign bank notifies Vinny that it will report his account information to IRS by the end of the year. Assume the bank account belonged to Vinny for many years, is located in his country of citizenship and tax returns have been filed in that country, although no taxes were paid on the interest income, because the country does not tax it. Vinny was never previously informed by his bank, a tax professional or anyone else that he needed to report his foreign income and accounts.

1. Doing nothing is not a realistic option, since it is just a matter of time until IRS discovers the situation, since under FATCA, the foreign account information must be produced upon an IRS request. OVDI offers immunity from criminal prosecution, but is very expensive and time-consuming. Under streamlined, the Vinny must certify he was non-willful under these circumstances, if IRS concludes otherwise, then all bets are off and he can be prosecuted for perjury and tax evasion.

a. Some of the issues that come to mind: Did Vinny have a professional tax preparer supply a tax questionnaire that asked about foreign accounts and did he indicate he did not. Were there email or correspondence about the foreign accounts? Did a tax preparer tell Vinny that he did not need to report the funds? Did Vinny use the funds in the account to for his benefit by withdrawing money through an ATM or debit card in the U.S. or elsewhere? How were the funds obtained, by an inheritance or gift, or were they earned by Vinny before he became a U.S. person? Were there investments being made and discussed with a financial advisor after Vinny became a U.S. taxpayer, i.e. how active was the account and were there unreported gains, in addition to the income?

b. In contrast, if the funds were inherited from Vinny's father with instructions that his mother should receive the income from the account during her life, and if mother had power of attorney over the account and Vinny never withdrew the funds for his benefit, these factors would indicate he was nonwillful in his failure to report the account and its income, because he considered it as belonging to his mother during the rest of her life.

c. Usually, there are factors pointing to both willfulness and non-willfulness, which makes the determination so difficult. Look for evidence of concealment, deceit or active control over the funds (investing, withdrawing the money), because if one or more of those factors are present, there is a strong indication of willfulness. Conversely, the absence of any of those factors would be consistent with Vinney acting non-willfully.

FAILURE TO DISCLOSE FOREIGN FINANCIAL ASSETS

d. Remember, on the issue of willfulness, the target audience is not Vinny or his advisor, it is a skeptical IRS agent who is probably already suspicious of someone with a foreign account. The ultimate decision-maker could be a jury in a criminal court trial, so Vinny needs to weigh the willfulness issue against the potential audience – would IRS or a jury believe him, based on the evidence?

e. If Vinny filed Schedule "B" of Form 1040, and checked the box "no" with respect to having foreign accounts, this could be a decisive factor, since IRS and the courts hone in on this as an act of affirmative deceit. There can be explanations why the box was checked "no", but when there are other significant factors indicating willfulness, a taxpayer should consider OVDP. It needs to be stressed that checking the box "no" is not fatal, but the issue must be emphasized and addressed in the analysis. Of course, if taxpayer checked the box "yes" as to foreign accounts, but failed to report the income or file FBARS, that is positive indication that he was trying to comply with the tax law and could be an important factor in concluding he was non-willful

Conclusion

The issue of willfulness has tax advisors scratching their heads, since it is a difficult concept to grasp and is fact intensive, with no two situations being the same For this reason, taxpayers should not enter the streamlined disclosure program without a thorough appreciation for the risk they are taking if they claim non-willfulness, especially when there are significant factors against them. Merely checking the box "no" as to foreign accounts, without more, does not rise to the level of willfulness, but when additional factors indicating the taxpayer engaged in concealment, deceit or active control over, or use of, the foreign funds, the streamlined procedures should not be used and the Draconian OVDP process becomes the only realistic alternative.

Appendix A

Outline for Streamlined Disclosure

I. Background

A. Create a timeline (dates on the left side and written description to the right of the dates) with:

1. Your date of birth, city and country, describe your family and what your parents did for a living.

2. Where your lived growing up.

3. The beginning and graduating dates of college.

4. The college name and decree.

5. Your job history before coming to the U.S. (dates, companies and positions).

6. When you came to the U.S.

7. Your visa status when you came to the U.S. and your subsequent visa/immigration status (including the month and year for each change).

   a) If you came as a student, the type of visa, the years, college and your degree.

   b) If you came on a work visa, the type(s) of visas the years, the companies you worked for and your job descriptions.realistic alternative.

II. Foreign assets, income and accounts

A. Foreign financial accounts – for each foreign account supply the following information:

1. The opening date.

2. The bank's name and country where it is located.

3. The circumstances for the account, for example:

   a) Joint account with a family member.

Appendix A

    b) You were living and working in the city and coun try where the account was opened.

    c) You used the account for business transactions in the country where the account is located.

B. Describe what happened to the account when you came to the U.S.

  1. Did you or someone else add money to the account from U.S. sources?

  2. Did you or someone else withdraw funds from the account? If so, how? – ATM, debit card?

  3. Were funds in the account used for a one-time purchase, such as the purchase of a home or rental property?

  4. Were funds in the account used to support a parent or relative?

  5. Did someone else have a power of attorney over the account?

C. Foreign Income

  1. Describe whether you earned income from overseas accounts, investments, rents, royalties or assets?

    a) If so, provided the year and dollar amounts of the foreign income earned.

    b) Did you report the income on your U.S. tax returns?

  2. Did you filed tax returns and paid taxes in the country where the money was earned? If, so describe the years and the country in which taxes were paid and how they were paid, for instance, by direct withholding or by filing tax returns and paying the taxes pursuant to the return.

Appendix A

D. Foreign Gift of Inheritance

1. If you received an inheritance or gift from a foreign person, describe the year, the asset (cash, real property, gold) and the approximate amount of each gift or inherited item. The term "person" includes corporations, trusts or other non-individual entities.

III. U.S. Taxpayer

A. Failure to File FBARS or Report Income

1. Describe when you became a U.S. taxpayer and, if applicable why you failed to file foreign bank account reports (FBARS).

2. Describe why you failed to report your foreign income on U.S. tax returns.

B. Willful vs. non-willful conduct:

1. In the Certification, you must state under federal laws of perjury that:

   a) Your failure to report all income, pay all tax, and submit all required information returns, including FBARs, was due to non-willful conduct;

   b) You understand that non-willful conduct is conduct that is due to negligence, inadvertence, or mistake or conduct that is the result of a good faith misunderstanding of the requirements of the law.

C. Examples of Willful Conduct

1. Obviously, if you deliberately failed to report income or file foreign bank account reports, or were advised to do so and refused, your conduct is willful.

2. Hiding assets in secret accounts or using sham entities, such as companies or trusts to hide your identity is willful conduct.

Appendix A

3. Having multiple passports and opening accounts with the foreign passport to avoid U.S. detection can also be viewed as willful behavior.

4. If you were using the accounts on a frequent basis and depositing and withdrawing funds or were engaged with an advisor regarding investing the funds – this also tends to show willful conduct.

5. If you received cash payments in a foreign country and carried them to another country (including the U.S.) either depositing them into an undisclosed foreign bank or your U.S. bank, but not reporting the income on your returns, this would be an example of willful conduct.

6. But what about failing to find out your responsibilities, i.e., were your "willfully blind" to your obligations?

   a) To establish willful blindness in the context of FBAR actions IRS will have to prove, at a mini mum, that the you subjectively believed that there was at least some requirement to report bank accounts and that you affirmatively avoided know ing the details of that requirement.

   b) Merely showing that you had knowledge that the income needed to be reported, or that there are generally reporting rules for certain overseas items, should not be sufficient.

   c) Failure to inquire simply does not equate with willful blindness. Furthermore, the IRS will have to prove that deliberate actions were taken by the you to avoid gaining confirmation of that subjective belief.

   d) In short, not knowing about the FBAR or foreign income reporting requirements and not taking actions to find out about them is not considered

Appendix A

willful blindness. There must be deliberate or evasive action to bring conduct within the willful blindness rules.

D. Examples of Non-Willful Conduct and Potential Reasons for Failing to Comply

The following are several potential reasons why you did not comply with the filing requirements:

1. Your tax preparer told you it was not necessary.

2. Your tax preparer never asked about foreign accounts; never asked about foreign income or assets, even though he/she was told that had had foreign income/business/assets.

3. Your tax preparer failed to advise you about the requirement.

4. Your tax preparer told you that only U.S. source income is reported and that if income is reported and taxed in a foreign country, it is not reported on U.S. returns.

5. You told you tax preparer (or provided him/her with foreign account statements), whom you relied on as my tax expert and he/she negligently failed to advise you about your foreign tax and reporting requirements and negligently failed to include the proper schedules with your tax returns.

6. You prepared your own returns and were never prompted about foreign accounts.

7. You did not attach Schedule B to Form 1040, so you were unaware of the foreign account requirement.

8. You prepared your own returns using software (such as Turbotax), and mistakenly checked the box "no" as to foreign accounts on Schedule B to Form 1040. Explain your mistake.

Appendix A

9. You prepared your returns but did not understand that you needed to report the foreign income/accounts.

10. You mistakenly thought that the U.S. was concerned with taxpayers forming foreign accounts with U.S. income and not all foreign bank accounts.

11. You did not really have ownership over the accounts (the accounts were held jointly with a family member; or a family member had power of attorney over the accounts and used the account to support himself/herself).

12. You were confused about the requirements since income was reported in the foreign country.

13. You misunderstood that your foreign income and assets, reported and taxed by the foreign country, were to be included on a U.S. tax return as well.

14. You were confused because the bank accounts were not related to U.S. income or assets.

15. You were confused about reporting world-wide income as opposed to just U.S. source-income and assets, when the foreign assets were acquired long before taxpayer became subject to U.S. taxes.

16. It never occurred to you that assets and income from your foreign country, which has been reported and taxed by your foreign country, would be subject to U.S. tax fling and reporting obligations as well.

E. You need to clearly explain what happened. This is critical to the Certification process.

1. When (the date) did you first learned about the requirement to file FBARS and report your foreign income?

Appendix A

2. How did you learned about it (a notice from a bank; something you read on the internet or in print; discussion with a friend or tax advisor).

3. Describe what steps you took to come into com-pliance, such as reading about the subject or consulting with a tax expert.

Appendix B

Certification by U.S. Person Residing in the United States for Streamlined Domestic Offshore Procedures
Attached Explanation

Personal Background

I am a U.S. citizen, with a couple of bank and investment accounts in India, my former country of citizenship. I opened these accounts for family investment as well as a source of travel funds within India.

Foreign Accounts and Reporting

My annual foreign income is roughly $200 U.S. I have not reported my foreign income nor financial accounts and I have several "passive foreign investment company" (PFIC) investments. The highest aggregate year-end amount in my foreign accounts was $155,550 in 2014 and I held in excess of $100,000 in my foreign accounts. Although my foreign bank entered into a FATCA agreement with the U.S., it, nevertheless, failed to send me income information or notify me about my U.S. filing obligations, thus, the bank is in violation of its duties under FATCA.

Non-Willful Conduct

My actions are considered non-willful because I:

(1) was never informed by a tax professional or anyone else about the FBAR and foreign income tax filing requirements;

(2) notified my foreign bank that I was a U.S. tax payer and requested that statements of income and gains be sent to my U.S. address;

(3) never received statements from my bank regarding my income or gains, thus causing me to erroneously conclude that I had no income or gains to report;

(4) just recently discovered my foreign income and

Appendix B

account reporting obligations in January, 2016, when I decided to close my foreign accounts and send the money to the U.S., and

(5) immediately consulted with an experienced U.S. tax attorney who advised me of my foreign tax filing obligations and decided to enter into the IRS SOVDP.

Dated: _____, 2016

_____
[Taxpayer]

Appendix B

Certification by U.S. Person Residing in the United States for Streamlined Domestic Offshore Procedures
Attached Explanation

I was born on May 1, 1970, in St. Petersburg, which was then USSR and is now Russia. My parents were both doctors in the USSR. I emigrated to the US in December 1988 on a refugee visa, then received my a green card and then became a US citizen in 2000. I never worked while in the US and was supported by my family. I moved back to Russia in 2005 and have not spent more than two week a year in the U.S. ever since. I have no income or earnings in the U.S. or elsewhere, as I am supported by my parents, due to my medical condition.

I opened an account in Swiss bank account August, 2010. The account was opened for my partner who is an musical performer and was going to study in the France. My partner needed someone to open an account for him and I did no. The funds in the account were his and after a few years, my name was removed from the account.

My failure to submit FBARs was due to non-willful conduct. I understand that non-willful conduct is conduct that is due to negligence, inadvertence, or mistake or conduct that is the result of a good faith misunderstanding of the requirements of the law.

I was not aware of the fact that I had to file FBARS and was not cognizant of foreign income filing requirements. I learned about the requirement in March, 2015 when the bank sent me a letter, and I immediately contacted an attorney and later a CPA and started the process.

Dated: _____, 2016

_____
[Taxpayer]

NOTES

16775216R00020

Made in the USA
Middletown, DE
26 November 2018